FIVE SHORT PLAYS

It's not always easy to know the right thing to do. For the people in these five short plays, life can be difficult and sometimes very funny.

Harry and his friends are fed up because they haven't got any money. But Harry has a plan to change all this. It's a good plan, but even the best plans can go badly wrong . . .

'Listen,' says Ron, 'My friend over there has got a gun. Give me the money! Give it to me now!'

'What money?' the woman answers. 'I'm sorry, this is not a bank. This is a library.'

Sid and Ron must steal something, but it isn't easy to rob a library. The woman happily gives them library cards so they can borrow books, and not steal them. In fact, she's very pleased to help . . .

Things are often more difficult than they seem. But as in all these plays, people are often more interesting, and much funnier, when they're trying to do the right thing.

OXFORD BOOKWORMS LIBRARY

Playscripts

Five Short Plays

Stage 1 (400 headwords)

Playscripts Series Editor: Clare West

MARTYN FORD

Five Short Plays

OXFORD UNIVERSITY PRESS

OXFORD

UNIVERSITY PRESS

Great Clarendon Street, Oxford OX2 6DP

Oxford University Press is a department of the University of Oxford.
It furthers the University's objective of excellence in research, scholarship,
and education by publishing worldwide in

Oxford New York

Auckland Cape Town Dar es Salaam Hong Kong Karachi
Kuala Lumpur Madrid Melbourne Mexico City Nairobi
New Delhi Shanghai Taipei Toronto

With offices in

Argentina Austria Brazil Chile Czech Republic France Greece
Guatemala Hungary Italy Japan Poland Portugal Singapore
South Korea Switzerland Thailand Turkey Ukraine Vietnam

OXFORD and OXFORD ENGLISH are registered trade marks of
Oxford University Press in the UK and in certain other countries

ISBN 978 0 19 423500 6

A complete recording of this Bookworms edition of
Five Short Plays is available.

Printed in China

Illustrated by: Rob Davis

For more information on the Oxford Bookworms Library,
visit www.oup.com/bookworms

CONTENTS

INTRODUCTION

This play is about a group of five friends. They are fed up because they haven't got any money. But this is all going to change soon. One of the group, Harry, has a plan – a very good plan.

CHARACTERS IN THE PLAY

Harry
Sid
Wilf
Gladys
Ron
Three people reading in a library
Woman working in a library

PERFORMANCE NOTES

Scene 1: A room in the friends' home. There are chairs and a table. Everything looks very old and dirty. Wilf and Gladys are drinking tea. Ron is looking out of the window. Sid is watching the television, but it is not working.

Scene 2: Inside a library. There is a woman sitting at a table. She works in the library. Three other people are standing or sitting, holding books in their hands and reading.

You will need a table, chairs, an old television, two library cards and some books.

The Robbery

The plan

Harry comes into the room. His friends look up at him.

HARRY Hello, everyone. What are you doing?

SID Nothing, Harry, nothing! What can we do? We haven't got any money.

HARRY I know, I know. But it's OK. I have some work for us. We can make a lot of money.

WILF Work? But you don't like work, Harry.

HARRY Ah, but this work is different.

GLADYS How, Harry? What are we going to do?

HARRY We're going to rob a bank.

GLADYS Rob a bank? But how can we?

HARRY I have a plan, a very good plan.

WILF Which bank are we going to rob?

HARRY The Capital Bank.

WILF Which one is that?

HARRY The one next to the library in the High Street.

SID That's a very big bank!

HARRY Be quiet and listen. Now, I want Wilf to drive the car, and Gladys to stand outside the bank and watch the street.

'I have a plan, a very good plan.'

WILF AND GLADYS   OK, Harry.

HARRY   Sid—

SID   (*Excitedly*) Yes, Harry? What do you want me to do?

HARRY   You must go into the bank and speak to everyone there. Say to them, 'Stay there! Don't move! I've got a gun in my pocket.'

SID   But Harry, we haven't got a gun.

HARRY   I know that! You just put your hand in your pocket like this. Move your hand up and down in your pocket and say, 'This is a gun!'

SID   I understand.

HARRY   Good. Now, Ron, I want you to go with Sid—

RON   Yes, Harry, and then what?

HARRY   Go to one of the bank workers and say, 'My friend has a gun. Give me the money!'

GLADYS   What are *you* going to do, Harry?

HARRY   I'm going to wait in the car with Wilf. Do you have any questions?

ALL   No.

HARRY   OK. So let's look at the plan again . . .

SCENE 2

The robbery

Sid and Ron run into the library. The people there look up from their books.

SID   Listen to me, all of you. This is a robbery. Don't move. I've got a gun in my pocket.

PEOPLE   Oh, don't shoot! Please don't shoot! We don't want to die.

SID   Nobody's going to die, but you must do what I say. (*To Ron*) Go on, Ron. What are you waiting for? Get the money! Quick!

Ron goes over to the woman who works there.

RON   Listen, my friend over there has got a gun. Give me the money! Give it to me now!

WOMAN What money?

RON What do you mean, 'What money?' The money in this bank, of course!

WOMAN I'm sorry, this is not a bank. This is a library.

RON What did you say – a library?

WOMAN That's right. People come here to borrow books. We don't have any money here.

RON Er, you don't have any money . . . Oh dear! . . . Sid! Sid!

SID What? Have you got the money?

RON There isn't any money. It's not a bank, Sid. We're not in a bank. This is a library!

SID A library?

RON That's right. They've only got books – lots and lots of books!

SID Books? Well, get some of those, then. We must take something, or Harry's going to be angry.

RON (*To the woman*) Give me lots of books!

WOMAN Have you got a library card?

RON A card? No, I haven't.

WOMAN I'm sorry, you can't borrow books without a library card.

RON Look, you don't understand, we're not *borrowing* books, we're *stealing* them!

WOMAN I'm sorry, but you can't do that.

RON Sid, we can't steal books, she says.

'Have you got a library card?'

SID   I've got a gun. Tell her that!

RON   My friend's got a gun and he knows how to shoot!

WOMAN Look, it's not a problem. I can give you and your friend a library card. Then you can borrow the books and not steal them. What are your names?

RON   Oh, all right. I'm Ronald Savage, and he's Sidney Dupree.

WOMAN (*Writing*) Ronald Savage . . . Sidney Dupree. And what's your address?

RON   27 Dunfore Road, Hamley.

WOMAN   (*Writing*) 27 Dunfore Road, Hamley. Good, here you are. (*She gives Ron two library cards.*) Now you can borrow some books.

RON   But I don't know anything about reading. You must help me. Which books are best?

SID   Quick, Ron! I can't stand here much longer.

WOMAN   Here are some good books for you. (*She takes three books from the shelves.*) *The Great Train Robbery*, *The Return of Sherlock Holmes*, and *The Adventures of Robin Hood*. They're all very famous books.

RON   Oh, that's nice. They look interesting. Thanks.

SID   Ron, come on! Quick!

RON   It's OK, Sid, I've got the books.

SID   All right. (*To the people in the library*) We're going now, but don't move. Don't move or talk for five minutes.

PERSON 1   Can we read?

SID   Er, all right. But you must read *quietly*, OK?

RON   Come on, Sid! Let's go. Harry and the others are waiting.

WOMAN   Goodbye, and happy reading!

RON   Oh yes, thank you. All right, Sid. I'm coming.

They run out of the library.

PERSON 2   Oh dear! I was so afraid!

WOMAN Oh, they weren't so bad. The one called Sid – he didn't really have a gun, you know.

PERSON 3 Perhaps. But they were robbers. They wanted to rob the bank!

WOMAN (*Laughing*) Yes, but they came into the wrong building!

PERSON 1 Why do you look so pleased?

WOMAN Well, it's important for everybody to read books – not just you and me, but *everybody* . . . even bank robbers!

PERSON 2 But you aren't going to get those books back, are you?

WOMAN Oh yes, I am. Remember, I've got their names and their address!

'Remember, I've got their names and their address!'

INTRODUCTION

In this play a man is lying in the street. Three different people stop and look. Perhaps the man needs help. But they don't know him, so it's not their problem, is it? Then a woman in blue arrives and suddenly things are different.

CHARACTERS IN THE PLAY

Patrick
Rebecca
David
Woman in blue
Michael Scott, a man lying in the street
Doctor
Nurse

PERFORMANCE NOTES

For this play you will need a small bottle of pills, a glass of water, blue clothes for the woman, a white coat for the doctor, and perhaps special clothes for the nurse.

The Right Thing to Do

A man is lying in the street. Rebecca is walking past. She stops and looks at him, then she looks around her – there is nobody there. She starts to walk away, stops, and goes back to look at the man again. Patrick walks past and stops to look at the man.

PATRICK What's the matter with him?
REBECCA I don't know.
PATRICK Is he dead?
REBECCA No, he's alive, I think.
PATRICK Are you going to help him?

'Is he dead?'

REBECCA Me? Why me?

PATRICK You were here first.

REBECCA Yes, I was, but—

David comes in.

DAVID What's the matter with him?

PATRICK We don't know.

DAVID He looks ill.

REBECCA His eyes are closed. Look!

DAVID Perhaps he's asleep.

REBECCA Asleep? In the street?

PATRICK Wake him up then.

DAVID Why me? You do it.

PATRICK (*To Rebecca*) What about you?

REBECCA Me?

PATRICK Yes. You were here first.

REBECCA Yes, but it's not my problem.

DAVID And it's not my problem!

A woman in blue comes in. She kneels down at once to help the man.

REBECCA Hey, what are you doing?

WOMAN I'm helping this man, of course!

DAVID Are you a doctor?

WOMAN No, I'm not, but he needs help.

REBECCA Do you know him?

WOMAN No, I don't.

REBECCA Then he's not your problem.

'Go and call an ambulance.'

WOMAN Oh, be quiet!

REBECCA (*To the others*) Did you hear that? She said, 'Be quiet!'

WOMAN Be quiet and help.

REBECCA She said it again!

WOMAN (*To David*) Go and call an ambulance.

DAVID Me?

WOMAN Yes, you. And be quick.

DAVID But—

WOMAN Be quick! (*David goes away.*) Now you – (*turning to Rebecca*) go and get some water.

REBECCA Where from?

WOMAN From that house over there. Don't look at me like that. Go!

REBECCA I'm going. (*Rebecca goes away.*)

WOMAN (*To Patrick*) Feel his pulse.

PATRICK But I—

WOMAN Go on! Feel his pulse.

PATRICK (*Kneeling down and taking the man's pulse*) Well, he's still alive. He's saying something!

WOMAN What is he saying?

PATRICK He said, 'Pills,' I think.

WOMAN (*To Patrick*) Pills? Look in his pocket.

PATRICK I can't do that!

WOMAN Look in his pocket!

Patrick looks in the man's coat pocket.

PATRICK There's a bottle with some writing on it.

WOMAN What does it say? Read it!

PATRICK It says, 'For the heart. If you feel ill, take one of these pills.'

Rebecca comes back with a glass of water.

REBECCA I've got the water.

WOMAN Good. (*To Patrick*) Give him one of the pills with some water.

Patrick helps the man to sit up. He gives him a pill and some water.

MAN (*Very quietly*) Thank you, thank you!

PATRICK How do you feel?

MAN A little better now.

The woman in blue goes away. The others do not see this. David comes running back.

DAVID   The ambulance is coming.

PATRICK   Good.

DAVID   How is he?

REBECCA   He's feeling a little better.

A doctor and a nurse come in. Patrick stands up.

DOCTOR   (*Kneeling down by the man*) What's the matter?

MAN   I was ill. It was my heart. That man gave me one of my pills. I'm all right now.

The doctor and the nurse help him to stand up.

NURSE   What's your name?

MAN   Scott. Michael Scott.

DOCTOR   Michael Scott, the famous TV chef?

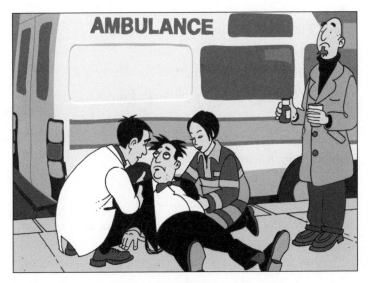

'What's the matter?'

MAN   Yes, that's right.

NURSE   Come with us, Mr Scott. We'd like to take you to hospital.

MAN   But I feel better now.

NURSE   Perhaps, but you must go to hospital.

MAN   All right. (*Turning to the others*) Well, thank you very much, everybody.

DAVID   That's all right.

REBECCA   We're happy to help.

PATRICK   Get well soon.

MAN   Thank you again. Goodbye!

The doctor and the nurse help Scott to walk away.

REBECCA   He's alive, and he's going to be OK.

PATRICK   He's alive because we were here.

DAVID   Michael Scott—

REBECCA   The famous TV chef!

PATRICK   We can all feel very pleased, I think.

REBECCA   Oh yes, we can.

DAVID   What about the woman?

REBECCA   Which woman?

DAVID   The woman who helped. Where is she?

PATRICK   Oh, *her*! I remember. She didn't help *us*.

DAVID   'Do this, do that,' she said. 'Be quick!'

REBECCA   She said, 'Be quiet,' to me.

PATRICK   That's right. I didn't like her. Did you?

REBECCA   No, I didn't. Where is she now?

'Well done, everybody!'

PATRICK She walked away.

DAVID That's right – she just walked away. She didn't want to help.

REBECCA We did everything.

DAVID Yeah. Everything.

PATRICK Today was an important day for us.

DAVID It was. We helped someone famous.

REBECCA Because of us he didn't die.

DAVID We were there for him.

PATRICK It was the right thing to do.

REBECCA Yes, it was. Well done, everybody!

DAVID (*To Rebecca*) And well done to *you*—

PATRICK Well done to all of us!

INTRODUCTION

This play is about a young person who wants to change his life. Chris would like to see new places and learn new things, but the older people in his life don't like his plan. They can only see problems. Chris finds that he, too, is a little afraid of change.

CHARACTERS IN THE PLAY

Chris, a young person who wants to travel

Cox
Mills
Harris } five of Chris's friends, all older than him
Dean
Wright

PERFORMANCE NOTES

At the beginning of the play Chris's friends are in a room. Cox is reading a book, Mills and Harris are talking quietly to each other, and Wright and Dean are looking out of a window. You will need six chairs, a book, a bag and a map.

Canada Can Wait

Cox, Mills and Harris are sitting in a room. Dean and Wright are standing by a window. Chris comes in.

CHRIS (*Smiling*) Well, goodbye, everyone.

COX (*Putting down his book*) Are you going?

CHRIS Yes, I must.

MILLS When are you going?

CHRIS Now.

'Well, goodbye, everyone.'

COX   Now? So soon?

MILLS   Don't go!

CHRIS   But I must. I need a change.

HARRIS   What are you going to do?

CHRIS   I'd like to travel for a time.

HARRIS   Travel? How wonderful!

DEAN   Yeah, think of us when you're travelling.

COX   Yes, think of us – we have to stay here.

MILLS   It's the same old thing, day after day—

HARRIS   The same old faces.

WRIGHT   The same old problems.

MILLS   Nothing different for us!

DEAN   But someone has to do it.

COX   Yes, that's right. We can't *all* go!

CHRIS   Why not? You can travel too.

COX   Us? (*He laughs.*)

MILLS   How can we travel?

HARRIS   We have things to do here.

CHRIS   What things?

WRIGHT   He says, 'What things?'

DEAN   What a question!

COX   (*To the others*) He's tired of us.

CHRIS   No, I'm not. I'm not tired of you. I'm happy here.

MILLS   Are you?

CHRIS   Well, I *was* happy here. It's a good place, and I—

HARRIS   Yes?

'Spain, perhaps, or Greece . . .'

CHRIS Well, I like you. I'm one of you – one of the group.

WRIGHT That's nice.

DEAN So where would you like to go?

CHRIS I don't know. Spain, perhaps, or Greece . . . maybe even Canada—

COX Canada?

CHRIS Yes. I'm very interested in Canada.

MILLS Canada, well!

HARRIS That's interesting.

WRIGHT You're very adventurous, Chris.

COX We're not adventurous at all, I'm afraid.

DEAN But then you're young—

19

'The lakes and the forests . . .'

COX   You have your life in front of you.

MILLS   You want to see exciting places—

HARRIS Like Canada!

WRIGHT The lakes and the forests . . .

COX   The great St. Lawrence River . . .

DEAN   How wonderful!

COX   Lucky Chris!

MILLS   It's different for us. We have to stay here. We can't go to Canada.

HARRIS 'I'm one of you,' you said, 'one of the group.' But you're not!

DEAN   No, Chris, you're different from us—

CHRIS   No, I'm not! Stop talking like this. I'm not different from you. Sometimes I'm happy, sometimes I'm not. I work and eat and sleep, like you.

MILLS   Ah, but *you* are going away—

HARRIS   And *we* are staying here.

WRIGHT   And that makes you different.

CHRIS   I'm *not* different!

COX   But what about Canada?

CHRIS   Stop talking about Canada! I'm not going to Canada – I'd *like* to go there, that's all!

COX   So you *aren't* going there now?

CHRIS   I don't know. Perhaps. I need some time to think about my life.

WRIGHT   Oh, yes.

DEAN   Everyone does.

MILLS   It's usual for people to do that.

HARRIS   And there's lots of time. You're young.

CHRIS   That's right. I have my life in front of me.

HARRIS   So, take your time.

CHRIS   Right.

WRIGHT   You can stay here as long as you like—

DEAN   And think about it.

CHRIS   Yeah. (*He sits down.*)

ALL   Mmm . . .

Everyone is quiet for a moment.

COX   So what are you going to do?

CHRIS   Sorry?

MILLS   Are you leaving today?

CHRIS   Leaving? Er, not today. I want to think about it first.

MILLS   Of course.

HARRIS   When are you going, then?

CHRIS   Well, not now. Later, perhaps. I can stay here a bit longer. There's lots of time. (*Laughing*) Canada can wait, can't it?

WRIGHT   Yes, it can. It certainly can!

DEAN   You're one of us really, aren't you, one of the group?

CHRIS   Yes, I am, I think.

COX   (*Laughing*) But, you know, you say—

CHRIS   Yes? Say what?

COX   Well, you say some funny things sometimes!

CHRIS   Like what?

COX   Well, *Canada!*

Cox, Mills, Harris, Dean and Wright all laugh.

CHRIS   (*Looking at them*) What's so funny about that?

MILLS   (*Laughing quietly*) It doesn't matter.

HARRIS   Forget it.

COX   Look at the time – I must go!

MILLS   Me too. I have a lot to do.

HARRIS   And me.

WRIGHT Let's all go.

DEAN Yes, let's leave Chris with his dreams—

COX About *Canada*!

They all laugh at Chris.

COX See you later, Chris.

ALL Bye-bye.

COX (*To Chris*) Bye-bye, traveller!

Chris's friends laugh, and then go out. Chris stands and watches them go. He doesn't look happy. He opens his bag and takes out a large map. He opens the map on the floor and looks at it carefully.

CHRIS Thailand . . . Malaysia . . . Indonesia . . . Australia
. . . (*He looks up, smiling.*) Mmm, Australia!

'Mmm, Australia!'

INTRODUCTION

A man goes into a grocery store and buys a lot of salt. At first the other people in the store can't understand why. Then they hear his story, and they all want to buy salt too.

CHARACTERS IN THE PLAY

Shopkeeper, a person who owns a small grocery store
Groot ⎫
Nello ⎪
⎬ four people in the grocery store
Durg ⎪
Spratly ⎭
Manra, a truck driver

PERFORMANCE NOTES

Scene 1: In a small grocery store.
Scene 2: In a street, some hours later.

You will need ten bags of salt, and a small cart on wheels. You will need the noise of a truck stopping suddenly, but we do not see the truck.

Salt

No more salt

In a small grocery store, Groot is asking the shopkeeper for something. The others are waiting behind him.

GROOT I'd like ten bags of salt, please.

SHOPKEEPER Ten? Of course. That's ten dollars, please.

GROOT Here you are.

SHOPKEEPER Can I help you with all that?

GROOT No, thanks. I have this cart.

SHOPKEEPER Ten bags. That's a lot of salt.

GROOT Yes. Salt is very important, you know.

SHOPKEEPER It is. But why do you need *ten* bags?

GROOT Soon there isn't going to be enough salt in the world. I saw it on television.

SHOPKEEPER Not enough salt? Really?

GROOT It's true. So I'm buying some now. Goodbye!

He goes out with his cart.

NELLO Did you hear that?

DURG Yeah, there isn't enough salt in the world.

SPRATLY Not enough salt? That isn't true.

NELLO But he saw it on television. Soon there isn't going to be any in the stores.

'Did you hear that?'

SPRATLY Really? That's bad – I need salt.

DURG Me too. I can't live without it!

NELLO (*To the shopkeeper*) Give me some salt, please, ten bags – no, make that twenty bags.

SPRATLY And me. I'd like thirty bags.

DURG Me first! I've got a big family. We need salt.

SHOPKEEPER Be quiet, all of you! You must wait.

NELLO But we want our salt.

DURG And we want it now.

SHOPKEEPER But that man bought my last ten bags.

SPRATLY Then it's true! He was right – there isn't enough salt in the world. What are we going to do?

SHOPKEEPER That's *your* problem. It's six o'clock – time to close the store. I'm going home.

NELLO But what about our salt?

SHOPKEEPER Look, there's a lot of salt in the world – enough for everybody. Goodbye!

They all go out.

SCENE 2
We want salt!

Spratly finds Groot standing in a street with his cart.

SPRATLY Excuse me, I want to buy some salt.

GROOT Sorry? What did you say?

SPRATLY I know about the problem.

GROOT What problem? What are you talking about?

SPRATLY Soon there isn't going to be enough salt.

GROOT Oh, you heard about that?

SPRATLY Yes, and I want some salt.

GROOT Then go to a grocery store and buy some.

SPRATLY I can't find any. Every time I ask, the shopkeeper says, 'Sorry, no more salt.'

GROOT Oh dear!

SPRATLY But *you* have some. You bought ten large bags – I saw you.

GROOT I'm sorry, but I'm not selling my salt.

'*But* you *have some.*'

SPRATLY But I'll give you ten dollars a bag.

GROOT (*Laughing*) No, I want fifty dollars a bag! It's more expensive every day. Soon there isn't going to be enough.

SPRATLY All right, all right, fifty dollars a bag! Give me five bags. Here's the money.

GROOT Good man! You're doing the right thing.

Spratly goes out. Durg comes in.

DURG Excuse me, I saw you buy some salt.

GROOT Ah!

DURG What's happening? I can't find any. The shopkeepers all say, 'Sorry. No more salt!'

28

GROOT   There's a problem.

DURG   I know. It was on television. Everybody is talking about it. Listen, I must have some salt.

GROOT   Sorry, I can't help you.

DURG   But I need it for my family. Please!

GROOT   All right, all right, but it's . . . er . . . a hundred dollars a bag.

DURG   Oh no!

GROOT   I told you – everybody wants salt. Well?

DURG   Oh, all right, then. Give me four bags.

GROOT   Four? Good! You understand the world, my friend. I see it in your face.

DURG   Here's the money.

GROOT   And here's your salt! Goodbye.

Durg goes out. Nello comes in.

NELLO   Hey, you, stop!

GROOT   Are you talking to me?

NELLO   Yes, you were in the grocery store—

GROOT   Was I? Perhaps. I go into a lot of grocery stores.

NELLO   You bought all the salt in the store!

GROOT   Well, there's a problem, you know.

NELLO   Yes, there is – and it's all because of you!

GROOT   That's not true!

NELLO   I met Spratly just now. He tried to sell me a bag of salt for five hundred dollars!

GROOT   That's too much.

Five Short Plays

NELLO   Of course it is – I know your plan! You go from store to store. You buy all the salt, and sell it for a lot more money!

GROOT   OK, it's true – I buy and sell salt – that's not wrong.

NELLO   Then sell some to me.

GROOT   No, I don't want to.

NELLO   (*Holding him, angrily*) Listen, I'm going to buy, and you're going to sell. (*Shouting*) Do you understand?

GROOT   But I've only got one bag left.

NELLO   (*Angrily*) Give it to me, then!

GROOT   It's two hundred dollars. Well, OK, you can have it for a hundred and fifty. But let me go!

NELLO   (*Shouting*) Give it to me!

GROOT   No, give me the money first. Now let me go! Oh, help! Help!

Groot runs out. We hear a truck stop suddenly, and Groot cries out. The driver, Manra, comes in, helping Groot to walk.

MANRA   He ran in front of my truck. I didn't see—

NELLO   You didn't do anything wrong. It was an accident.

MANRA   But why did he run across the street without looking?

NELLO   I was angry with him. So he ran away.

MANRA   (*To Groot*) How do you feel?

30

'He ran in front of my truck.'

GROOT (*Holding his leg*) Oh, my leg! My leg hurts. I think it's—

NELLO He's OK, I think.

MANRA Wait a minute, what's this in the street?

NELLO It's salt. He had a bag of salt and I wanted it.

MANRA Salt? Well, that's interesting! I'm carrying salt on my truck – bags and bags of it!

NELLO Salt? Oh no! (*He laughs.*)

MANRA Why are you laughing?

NELLO It doesn't matter. I can't tell you now.

MANRA Then you can tell that policeman. Look, he's coming across the street now. He saw the accident, I think!

INTRODUCTION

Maggie works in a fast-food restaurant. People come here to buy food when they haven't got much time. The restaurant sells 'fast food' – things like pizza, burgers, chicken and sandwiches. Five angry people are waiting for their food.

CHARACTERS IN THE PLAY

Maggie, a young woman who works in a fast-food restaurant

Two men } people who want to buy some food to eat
Three women

PERFORMANCE NOTES

In the window there is a sign saying, 'Fast Food'. There are some tables and chairs, and a large high counter. Maggie is standing behind this counter. The people in the restaurant are standing in front of it. They are wearing outdoor clothes. Maggie is wearing work clothes. She also needs a bag.

Slow Food

MAN 1   Excuse me, is my food ready?

MAGGIE   What did you ask for?

MAN 1   I asked for chicken.

MAGGIE   Er, let's see. Another five minutes.

MAN 1   Five minutes?

MAGGIE   Sorry, ten minutes.

MAN 1   Ten? That's no good! I must go back to my office in ten minutes.

MAN 2   And what about *my* food? I asked for a burger and French fries fifteen minutes ago!

'I asked for a burger and French fries fifteen minutes ago!'

MAGGIE   I'm sorry, but there are a lot of people eating here today.

MAN 2   But how long is it going to take? My train leaves in forty minutes.

MAGGIE   Not long. I'm very sorry.

WOMAN 1   Excuse me, I was before these men. Where is my coffee?

WOMAN 2   And what about me? I asked for a sandwich and a coke half an hour ago.

WOMAN 3   Well, I'm before all of you. I asked for a pizza forty-five minutes ago.

MAN 1   Look here, in your window it says, 'Fast food'.

MAGGIE   Yes, it does.

MAN 1   Then why is it so slow?

MAGGIE   It isn't slow. But people today want everything faster and faster—

MAN 1   What are you talking about?

WOMAN 1   Look, I can't wait. I have to get back to work.

WOMAN 2   And I have a meeting. I'm late.

MAN 2   Time is money, you know!

WOMAN 3   Where's my pizza?

WOMAN 1   Where's my coffee?

MAN 1   What about my chicken?

PEOPLE   We want our food!

MAGGIE   Please, everybody! Please! Your food is coming. He's doing it now.

'We want our food!'

PEOPLE *He?*

MAGGIE Sorry, *they.* The chefs are doing it now.

MAN 2 How many chefs have you got?

MAGGIE Oh, lots.

WOMAN 2 How many?

MAGGIE Some.

WOMAN 1 How many exactly? Tell us!

MAGGIE Er, twelve.

WOMAN 3 Your restaurant has twelve chefs?

MAGGIE Well, no, not now. We had one in January, one in February, one in March – one every month for the last year. That makes twelve.

WOMAN 3 Well, where are they now?

'Your restaurant has twelve chefs?'

MAGGIE They all stopped working here.

WOMAN 1 Why did they leave?

MAGGIE Because it was too fast for them.

MAN 2 And how many chefs have you got now?

MAGGIE Well, er . . . one.

PEOPLE One!

MAGGIE No, sorry. That's wrong—

MAN 1 I'm happy to hear it!

MAGGIE We haven't got *any.*

PEOPLE What?

MAGGIE That's right. There's only me here. Our last chef
        left yesterday. He was fed up with fast food.

MAN 2 Fed up?

MAGGIE Yes. He said to me, 'That's it! Enough! No more fast food for me! I'm going!' And he went.

WOMAN 2 But what about our—

MAGGIE And do you know? I'm fed up too. Yes, I'm really, really fed up. Fast chicken, fast burgers, fast French fries, fast coke, fast coffee, fast talking, fast walking, fast eating, fast sleeping, fast living, fast dying! I'm fed up with it all!

WOMAN 1 But who is going to—

MAGGIE What's the matter with everybody these days? Why is everything so fast? Come here. (*Maggie walks to the window.*) Come on! (*The people all go to the window.*) Look outside. Go on, look! It's a beautiful day. Life is beautiful. We can all be happy. But first we must slow down. We must take the time to *live.*

MAN 1 Live? But we have to work!

WOMAN 3 We have lots to do.

WOMAN 1 And we want food.

MAN 2 We want *fast* food—

WOMAN 1 Not *slow* food!

WOMAN 2 We haven't got time to—

MAGGIE Time! Time! Time! Don't talk to me about time. You don't understand it. You – oh, it's no good, you're not listening to me.

She takes off her work clothes and picks up a bag.

WOMAN 3   Hey, where are you going?

MAGGIE   I'm going out. I'm going to sit in the sun. I'm going to look at the sky and listen to the sea. I'm going to do nothing . . . *slowly*!

WOMAN 1   But what about our food?

MAN 2   What about my burger?

MAGGIE   *You* can do it!

MAN 2   *What* did you say?

MAGGIE   I said, you can do it. Behind me is the kitchen. In the kitchen there's a big bag of chicken and another bag of burgers. You can do your own food, and you can do it as fast as you like. Goodbye!

PEOPLE   But we don't—

MAGGIE   And have a nice day!

She goes out.

'We must take the time to live.'

GLOSSARY

adventurous of someone who likes doing exciting and
  dangerous things

asleep of someone who is sleeping; not awake

bank a place that keeps money safe for people

borrow to take and use something that you are going to give
  back after a short time

buy (past tense **bought**) to give money to get something

counter a long high table in a shop or a restaurant that is
  between the people who work there and the people who want
  to buy things

dream a hope for something nice in the future

fed up of someone who is not happy or who is bored because
  they have or do too much of something

funny of something that makes you laugh; of something that is
  not usual or is different

grocery store a building where people buy food and other small
  things for the home

group a number of people together

gun a thing that shoots out bullets to hurt or kill people

heart the thing inside the body that makes the blood go round

kneel down (past tense **knelt down**) to go down on your knees

library a place where you go to borrow or read books

library card a piece of plastic from a library with your name on
  it; you use it to borrow books

nurse a person who helps people who are sick or hurt

pill a small, round, hard medicine that you swallow

pizza a round, flat, Italian bread

plan something that you are going to do, and how you are going to do it

problem something that is difficult

restaurant a place where people buy food and eat it

rob to take things that are not yours from a bank, train (or other places) or people

robbery taking things that are not yours from a bank, train (or other places) or people

salt white stuff that comes from sea water; we put it on food to make it taste better

sell (past tense **sold**) to give something to somebody who pays you money for it

shoot (past tense **shot**) to send a bullet from a gun to hurt or kill someone

steal (past tense **stole**) to take something that is not yours

take (past tense **took**) **someone's pulse** to feel the beating of the heart in the wrist (or the neck)

travel to visit other countries

TV chef a person who cooks food on television

wake up to stop sleeping

world where we all live; people live in lots of different countries in the world

Five Short Plays

ACTIVITIES

Before Reading

1 **Here are the five play titles. Which of the five characters and five things below belongs to each play? Can you guess?**

The Robbery	a shopkeeper	a map
The Right Thing To Do	an office worker	a pizza
Canada Can Wait	a traveller	a bottle of pills
Salt	a TV chef	a library card
Slow Food	a nurse	fifty dollars

2 **There is a character called Chris in *Canada Can Wait*. What can you guess about him?**

1 He wants to *work in* / *visit* Canada.
2 Canada is the *only place* / *one of the places* he wants to visit.
3 His *friends* / *family* want to go to Canada.

3 **One of the plays is called *Slow Food*. What do you think this means? Circle Y (Yes) or N (No) for each answer.**

Food …
1 which is bad for you. Y / N
2 which everybody likes. Y / N
3 which takes a long time to grow. Y / N
4 which people need time to enjoy. Y / N

4 The first play is called *The Robbery*. Can you guess what is going to happen in this play? Use the words below to make some sentences about your guesses.

Harry	watches for	Sid and Ron
Ron	waits outside	the robbers
Gladys	helps them to	the police
Wilf	wants to rob	with his gun
Sid	shoots someone	in the car
The police	asks for	borrow books
Other people	catch	a bank
The woman in the library	fight with	the money

5 At the beginning of the second play, *The Right Thing to Do*, a man is lying in the street. What is going to happen? Can you guess? Tick one box for each sentence.

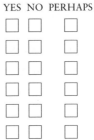

	YES	NO	PERHAPS
1 Everybody walks past him.	☐	☐	☐
2 Some people stop and try to help.	☐	☐	☐
3 A doctor calls an ambulance.	☐	☐	☐
4 A friend takes him to hospital.	☐	☐	☐
5 Someone steals his watch.	☐	☐	☐
6 He wakes up and walks home.	☐	☐	☐

ACTIVITIES

While Reading

Read *The Robbery*. Are these sentences true (T) or false (F)?

1 When Harry arrives, his friends are working hard.
2 Harry wants them to rob a rich old lady.
3 Harry teaches Sid to shoot.
4 Wilf is going to put the money in a safe place.
5 Sid likes Harry's plan very much.

Before you read Scene 2, can you guess what happens?

1 Harry tells the police about the robbery.
2 The robbers fight with each other over the money.
3 There is no money to steal.

Read *The Right Thing To Do*. Who says these words? Who are they talking to? And who or what are they talking about?

1 'Is he dead?'
2 'Why me? You do it.'
3 'He's not your problem.'
4 'It was my heart.'
5 'Where is she now?'
6 'We were there for him.'

44

Read *Canada Can Wait*. Then circle the correct words in each sentence.

1 At the beginning Chris *wants / doesn't want* to leave.
2 Chris's friends think that he is *tired of / happy with* them.
3 They want to see Canada's *cities / lakes and forests*.
4 They have to *visit Canada / stay at home*.
5 At the end they all *laugh / shout* at Chris.

Read *Salt*, and then put this summary into the right order. Start with number 3.

1 Groot and Nello start fighting.
2 The shopkeeper closes the store.
3 Groot buys ten bags of salt from the shop.
4 Manra's truck hits Groot.
5 Spratly buys five bags of salt for $250.
6 Spratly tries to sell a bag of salt to Nello.
7 Durg buys four bags of salt for $400.

Read *Slow Food*, pages 32 to 34. Underline the mistakes in this paragraph and then correct them.

On the counter there is a sign saying 'Slow Food'. Maggie is sitting at one of the tables. The first man is asking for a pizza. The second man wants chicken and French fries – he has to catch a bus in forty minutes. The three women are only waiting for drinks. They are all sorry for Maggie, because the food is so bad. Maggie loves her work.

After Reading

1 Match these halves of sentences to make a summary of *The Robbery*. Use these words to join the sentences.

because   but   or   so   when

1 Sid and Ron wanted to steal some money,

2 Sid said, 'I've got a gun in my pocket,'

3 They couldn't steal any money,

4 They didn't want Harry to be angry,

5 The woman in the library can write to Sid and Ron,

6 . . . they weren't in a bank.

7 . . . she wants the books back.

8 . . . perhaps steal some books.

9 . . . they borrowed some books.

10 . . . the woman in the library wasn't afraid.

2 Here are some new titles for the five plays. Which titles go with which plays? Which titles do you prefer? Why?

Fast Living	*Home's Best*	*Harry's Plan*
Get Well Soon!	*The Man With the Cart*	*The Dreamer*
Time is Money	*Bad Hearts and Good*	
The Right Price	*The Wrong Building*	

3 Use the clues below to complete this crossword with words from *The Right Thing to Do*. (All the words go across.)

1 The liquid in rivers, seas and lakes. (5)

2 The thing in the body that makes the blood go round. (5)

3 A glass or plastic container for holding pills. (6)

4 The opposite of dead. (5)

5 Someone whose job is to make ill people well again. (6)

6 Well known. (6)

7 A special car or van which carries people to hospital. (9)

8 A small bag in your clothes for carrying things. (6)

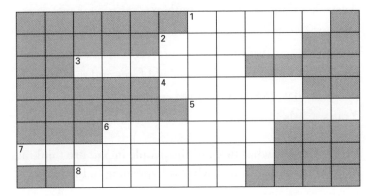

Can you find the two hidden words in the crossword?

1 What are the words?

2 Who said them, and why?

4 In *Canada Can Wait*, perhaps Chris wrote this letter to his friends the next day. Complete his letter with the groups of words below.

about it, exciting places, funny things, have to stay,
in front of, tired of, try to stop, have a dream

Dear friends,

I'm leaving tomorrow. Please don't _____ me. I'm not going because I'm _____ you; I'm going because I want to travel. I'm young and I have my life _____ me. I want to see _____, like Greece, Spain, and Australia. Canada can wait, perhaps, but not for me! Perhaps I do say _____ sometimes, but it's important to _____, isn't it? *You* can travel too, you know. You don't _____ with the same old faces and the same old problems day after day. Think _____!

Yours, Chris

5 Perhaps this is what three of the people in *Salt* are thinking. Who are the people, and what is happening in the play?

1 'Ah, good, time to go home. Chicken for dinner tonight, I think. I must remember to get some more salt tomorrow.'

2 'Oh no! Is he dead? No, he's getting up – I haven't killed him! Why did he run into the road like that? Hey – you!'

3 'I'm going to find that man and tell him what I think of him! I know his little plan. And I'm going to have some of his salt too!'

48

6 In *Slow Food,* perhaps Maggie writes an e-mail to her friend, Dave, the day after leaving her job. Use these words to complete her e-mail. (Use each word once.)

burger, chef, clothes, everything, food, restaurant, sea, work, yesterday

Hi Dave

Guess what! _____ I left my job at the fast food _____! You see, I had to do _____ there, even the cooking, because the _____ left the day before. Everybody wanted their _____ so fast! I couldn't stay there any longer. So I took off my work _____ and just walked out. I went to sit by the _____, and looked at the sky, and felt a lot better. I'm going to look for some different _____ tomorrow – I never want to see a _____ again!

See you, Maggie

7 Do you agree (A) or disagree (D) with these ideas from the five plays? Explain why.

1 You must never walk past someone lying in the street.
2 It is important for everyone to have a dream.
3 People must learn to slow down and enjoy life more.
4 It is wrong to make a lot of money from buying and selling things.

ABOUT THE AUTHOR

Martyn Ford has worked in English Language Teaching since 1980. He has been a teacher, teacher trainer and materials writer, and has taught in England, Italy and Switzerland. He is also a successful cartoon illustrator, and has illustrated several English language books as well as humorous books about Britain. With Peter Legon he has written and illustrated *The How To Be British Collection*.

He is particularly interested in the use of drama in language learning, and the plays in this book developed out of scripts which he wrote especially for the classroom. He would like to dedicate *Five Short Plays* to all the brave students who tried them out!

He lives and works in Brighton, on the south-east coast of England.

OXFORD BOOKWORMS LIBRARY

Classics • Crime & Mystery • Factfiles • Fantasy & Horror
Human Interest • Playscripts • Thriller & Adventure
True Stories • World Stories

The OXFORD BOOKWORMS LIBRARY provides enjoyable reading in English, with a wide range of classic and modern fiction, non-fiction, and plays. It includes original and adapted texts in seven carefully graded language stages, which take learners from beginner to advanced level. An overview is given on the next pages.

All Stage 1 titles are available as audio recordings, as well as over eighty other titles from Starter to Stage 6. All Starters and many titles at Stages 1 to 4 are specially recommended for younger learners. Every Bookworm is illustrated, and Starters and Factfiles have full-colour illustrations.

The OXFORD BOOKWORMS LIBRARY also offers extensive support. Each book contains an introduction to the story, notes about the author, a glossary, and activities. Additional resources include tests and worksheets, and answers for these and for the activities in the books. There is advice on running a class library, using audio recordings, and the many ways of using Oxford Bookworms in reading programmes. Resource materials are available on the website <www.oup.com/bookworms>.

The *Oxford Bookworms Collection* is a series for advanced learners. It consists of volumes of short stories by well-known authors, both classic and modern. Texts are not abridged or adapted in any way, but carefully selected to be accessible to the advanced student.

You can find details and a full list of titles in the *Oxford Bookworms Library Catalogue* and *Oxford English Language Teaching Catalogues*, and on the website <www.oup.com/bookworms>.

STARTER • 250 HEADWORDS

present simple – present continuous – imperative –
can/cannot, must – *going to* (future) – simple gerunds ...

Her phone is ringing – but where is it?

Sally gets out of bed and looks in her bag. No phone. She looks under the bed. No phone. Then she looks behind the door. There is her phone. Sally picks up her phone and answers it. *Sally's Phone*

STAGE 1 • 400 HEADWORDS

... past simple – coordination with *and, but, or* –
subordination with *before, after, when, because, so* ...

I knew him in Persia. He was a famous builder and I worked with him there. For a time I was his friend, but not for long. When he came to Paris, I came after him – I wanted to watch him. He was a very clever, very dangerous man. *The Phantom of the Opera*

STAGE 2 • 700 HEADWORDS

... present perfect – *will* (future) – *(don't) have to, must not, could* –
comparison of adjectives – simple *if* clauses – past continuous –
tag questions – *ask/tell* + infinitive ...

While I was writing these words in my diary, I decided what to do. I must try to escape. I shall try to get down the wall outside. The window is high above the ground, but I have to try. I shall take some of the gold with me – if I escape, perhaps it will be helpful later. *Dracula*

... should, may – present perfect continuous – *used to* – past perfect –
causative – relative clauses – indirect statements ...

Of course, it was most important that no one should see
Colin, Mary, or Dickon entering the secret garden. So Colin
gave orders to the gardeners that they must all keep away
from that part of the garden in future. ***The Secret Garden***

STAGE 4 • 1400 HEADWORDS

... past perfect continuous – passive (simple forms) –
would conditional clauses – indirect questions –
relatives with *where/when* – gerunds after prepositions/phrases ...

I was glad. Now Hyde could not show his face to the world
again. If he did, every honest man in London would be proud
to report him to the police. ***Dr Jekyll and Mr Hyde***

STAGE 5 • 1800 HEADWORDS

... future continuous – future perfect –
passive (modals, continuous forms) –
would have conditional clauses – modals + perfect infinitive ...

If he had spoken Estella's name, I would have hit him. I was so
angry with him, and so depressed about my future, that I could
not eat the breakfast. Instead I went straight to the old house.
Great Expectations

STAGE 6 • 2500 HEADWORDS

... passive (infinitives, gerunds) – advanced modal meanings –
clauses of concession, condition

When I stepped up to the piano, I was confident. It was as if I
knew that the prodigy side of me really did exist. And when I
started to play, I was so caught up in how lovely I looked that
I didn't worry how I would sound. ***The Joy Luck Club***

The Murder of Mary Jones

TIM VICARY

The court room is full for today's trial. Two young men, Simon Clark and Dan Smith, stand up. The clerk asks, 'Are you guilty of the murder of Mary Jones?' 'Not guilty!' they reply. But perhaps they *are* guilty. The police found the murder weapon in their stolen car, and there was blood on Simon's face. If the court finds them guilty, they will go to prison for a very long time.

Can the lawyers find out the truth, by asking the right questions? Everyone in court wants to know who murdered Mary Jones, especially her mother, and her boyfriend, Jim. *You* can help to find the answer, too!

A Ghost in Love and Other Plays

MICHAEL DEAN

Do you believe in ghosts? Jerry doesn't. He's a nineteen-year-old American, who just wants a good holiday with his friend, Brad. They are travelling round the north of England by bicycle. But strange things begin to happen in the small hotel where they are staying. First, Brad seems to think that he has been there before. And then a girl called Ellen appears . . .

The first of these three original plays is set in the seventeenth century, and the other two take place in modern times. In each play, a ghost comes back from the dead to change the lives of living people.

The Importance of Being Earnest

OSCAR WILDE

Retold by Susan Kingsley

Algernon knows that his friend Jack does not always tell the truth. For example, in town his name is Ernest, while in the country he calls himself Jack. And who is the girl who gives him presents 'from little Cecily, with all her love'?

But when the beautiful Gwendolen Fairfax says that she can only love a man whose name is Ernest, Jack decides to change his name, and become Ernest forever. Then Cecily agrees to marry Algernon, but only if his name is Ernest, too, and things become a little difficult for the two young men.

This famous play by Oscar Wilde is one of the finest comedies in the English language.

One Thousand Dollars and Other Plays

O. HENRY

Retold by John Escott

Money or love? Which is more important in life? Can money buy anything? Can it help a young man to marry the girl he loves? Does money really make people happy, or does it just cause problems?

We all know how difficult love can be. When you meet someone you like, there are so many things that can go wrong, sometimes because you are trying too hard, sometimes because of a misunderstanding.

These four plays about money, love and life are adapted from short stories written a hundred years ago by the great American storyteller O. Henry. Henry had his own difficulties with money and loneliness, and wrote from personal experience.

The Wizard of Oz

L. FRANK BAUM

Retold by Rosemary Border

Dorothy lives in Kansas, USA, but one day a cyclone blows her and her house to a strange country called Oz. There, Dorothy makes friends with the Scarecrow, the Tin Man, and the Cowardly Lion.

But she wants to go home to Kansas. Only one person can help her, and that is the country's famous Wizard. So Dorothy and her friends take the yellow brick road to the Emerald City, to find the Wizard of Oz . . .

Stories from the Five Towns

ARNOLD BENNETT

Retold by Nick Bullard

Arnold Bennett is famous for his stories about the Five Towns and the people who live there. They look and sound just like other people, and, like all of us, sometimes they do some very strange things. There's Sir Jee, who is a rich businessman. So why is he making a plan with a burglar? Then there is Toby Hall. Why does he decide to visit Number 11 Child Row, and who does he find there? And then there are the Hessian brothers and Annie Emery – and the little problem of twelve thousand pounds.